STRENGTH
AND
SIMPLICITY

STRENGTH
AND
SIMPLICITY

100 WAYS
TO
LIVE YOUR LIFE
AS
ART

KEVIN CALICA

STRONG AND SIMPLE PRESS
New York, New York

Published by STRONG AND SIMPLE PRESS

For inquiries:

STRONG AND SIMPLE PRESS
41 East 11th Street 11th Floor
New York, NY 10003
www.strengthandsimplicity.com

Distributed by Epigraph Publishing Service

978-1-936940-59-2
Library of Congress Control Number: 2013948583

TABLE OF CONTENTS

STRENGTH AND SIMPLICITY

STRENGTH AND SIMPLICITY
AN INTRODUCTION

When something is strong, it has impact and makes a difference; when something is simple, it has a basic, inherent ease. Since I never considered myself strong, I pursued a life strong in accomplishment and achievement in the hope of absorbing that quality. And since ease had always eluded me, I practiced listening to myself and so, began to discover the quality of simplicity.

Yet this didn't happen overnight nor did it happen without my time and intention.

Each and every day between the years of 2001 and 2003, the emptiness of my life seemed to increase. I found myself questioning everything I did. I was at a loss because very little I did had any real meaning to me. I was tired—not physically, but mentally. So after fifteen years of post-college life—struggling and striving—I decided to unplug.

I quit my job as a very successful fashion executive at the "apex" of my career. Friends and family witnessed this event in the same way you might watch a slow motion video of an on-coming car crash—with great concern and respectful silence.

I stopped everything and moved to Florida to be with my partner, and what followed was six months of basking in the sun, playing house and getting physically fit. I swam in the ocean like I was a child and I enjoyed the unfamiliarity of doing things in an unhurried manner. I savored long walks on the beach, and tended to my home with a care that had been foreign to me. This slower "pace" was a delicious revolution, a "game-changer."

The less I did, the more full I felt and this recognition was both stunning and alarming. It made me rethink everything I considered to be true. My rules got washed away with the tide. Think about having the structure of a lined notebook page swiftly replaced with an unlined drawing pad. *Crash, boom, bam!* Identity crisis!

Rather than sitting around on a pool chaise and being uncomfortable in paradise, I decided to plunge into my spiritual practices of meditation and community service with total abandon. Since I had given up so many other things that had filled my daily life, there was now nothing to stop me from moving forward on my spiritual path—which to me meant going deeper inside myself.

It was like diving into and under the gorgeous turquoise waters of Southern Florida, with no plans or even a desire to emerge anytime soon. Submerged, immersed, I called on every resource I had—career coach, life coach, mystical coach. I listened to what each one of them advised and I allowed myself to digest every morsel of wisdom. Yet nothing sated my appetite. A kind of collapse had begun. It was inward, not outward. My radiant tan, fit body and perfect relationship seemed to demonstrate that I was "living the dream," but those close to me knew otherwise. And so did I.

Later that summer, we were hit with not one but two hurricanes. The first landed down the road from where I had just purchased a new condominium, and the other, about an hour further south. Whatever wasn't securely fastened down got blown away. Many lost their homes and belongings; I was in the process of losing my old ideas and concepts. My comfort zone evaporated like the morning dew on a car's sunbaked hood.

Whatever I held on to ended up biting me. "Honeymoon" became "good-bye honey" and I got what I most feared—being alone. Having no choice but to keep moving forward, I went deeper inside and, with absolutely no distractions or the strength to make up excuses, I began to have a talk with myself—and not the way some people mutter while walking down the street. Mine was an inner dialogue.

I started by truly studying myself. Bit by bit, I was able to watch what I was doing and how I did it. After a while, it became less like work and more like research. I guess I never felt safe enough to let myself be curious and to not have to know everything. Slowly, slowly, by doing things more slowly, I felt better and more optimistic, almost like I'd put on a new suit of clothes called "confidence."

First out of necessity and, eventually, out of delight, I learned to enjoy the inward plunge. I began to thrive on the freshness of each moment rather than needing to plan it out. Wrapped in the embrace of my new potential, I was able to trust myself enough to feel the inevitable warmth that follows the re-ignition of the engine.

When I consider that period, now ten years past, I am humbled and awed at having had the courage to pull myself and my life out of the normal day-to-day mechanical survival mode that most of us don't even know we're in. By simplifying my life, I became stronger. After leaving the safety net of my old house, I walked into a new one full of real beauty and natural generosity.

To remind myself of what I relearned, I wrote this book. In it, I honor and mark the moments of my day in ways that provide beauty, order, measure, ritual and now, a delightful tradition. I've designed my life according to ten basic functions: SLEEPING, COOKING, EATING, DRESSING, COMMUTING, WORKING, FRIEND-ING, DECORATING, RESTING and THINKING.

What follows are 100 small yet significant changes I made that have worked wonders in my life. They've helped to make it strong and simple. I share them with love in the hope that, whether you use them as they are or make refinements to them, they inspire you to work the same magic in your own.

KC
NYC
August 1, 2013

CHAPTER 1

SLEEPING

1. Press your pillowcases

I won't lie to you and say I do this every time I change my sheets, but whenever I do, I notice a difference. Ironed pillowcases make a bed look crisp and feel neat and clean.

Think of the difference between wearing a pressed shirt and a wrinkled one right out of the dryer. Night and day!

When I take the time to pull out the iron and ironing board, I am always surprised at how little effort it takes to make those pillowcases special. I think the pillowcases enjoy it, too—it's like they're getting dressed up for a special occasion.

While ironing, I use water infused with lavender oil. The water makes it easy to cover a lot of the fabric and the rich, thick fragrance of the lavender oil is cool and very calming. It seeps into the cotton and I enjoy this scent throughout the week.

As I inhale the fragrance I imagine vast fields of lavender from an Impressionist's painting. The five minutes that it takes me to iron my pillowcases give me a few moments to get quiet and focus on something else besides what's on my desk or in my inbox.

When I get quiet, I feel good inside. And when I feel good inside, I feel strong. It's that simple.

2. Start winding down about two hours before sleep

When I first heard this piece of advice, I thought the person giving it was insane. I was brought up to utilize every millisecond of my "free time" to do something "important," or at least useful. Just the thought of this concept felt indulgent, but as I started to do it two hours before bed, I noticed that the quality of my sleep really improved!

Now, I think about gradually slowing the pace of my evenings in the same way I stretch after exercise to avoid cramping up.

I've come to really cherish this time. It has reframed my evenings and forced me to make more conscious choices about how I'm spending them: what I choose to do, and whom I do it with.

3. Have a beautiful image within sight of your bed

I've been doing this ever since I was a child.

I would position the blinds to let in the moonlight or just gaze at a poster on my wall. What I looked at right before closing my eyes would be my last memory of that day.

Back then, I had naïve expectations for the following day. It was almost like, by sleeping, I was putting the movie of my life on pause. Then—*voila!*—morning appeared and the movie would continue.

Even now I find that this evening tradition helps me to experience that same sense of wonder, stillness and pause. As I fall asleep, my last memory is filled with something attractive and dear to me. Looking at it transports me somewhere else and gets me ready for sleep.

When I wake up in the morning, I turn and, if I need to, focus on the same sight.

I find it makes me feel comforted and safe.

4. Sleep seven to nine hours

I know that for some, this goal seems completely unreachable, but I myself can't function at 100% without two things: 1) enough food, and 2) enough sleep.

Most Americans get about five hours of sleep a night. From the expressions on the faces of the people that I see in the morning, I would say that this is true, and it's clearly not enough. These people look sleep-starved.

This lack of nourishment affects every part of our lives. If I'm having problems sleeping, I know I'm having problems in my life. It's that simple. It's so easy to see ourselves as machines since our days are filled with them—computers, cellphones, GPS's and televisions—but we're living, breathing beings, not machines. If I'm having problems sleeping, I put four bags of chamomile tea in a mug of hot water and drink this in the mid-afternoon, and then again in the early evening.

Chamomile is a natural sedative. It calms the nerves and quiets the mind.

5. Use a traditional alarm clock

Remember those old things? A traditional alarm clock that gives you only one opportunity to snooze? And I don't put it on my bedside table. I put it on a dresser on the other side of my room, making sure I can see it easily and that I have to get out of bed to turn it off. Once my feet are on the floor, I'm up, and it seems almost sacrilegious to go back to bed.

The soft, red glow of the squared-off numbers reminds me of my youth. I find the sound of the alarm charming because it's so different from the sounds of *swooshes, dings, tings* and *harps* that my other devices emit throughout the day.

I enjoy doing things differently. It's refreshing and I consider it a form of strength and confidence.

6. Use a duvet with no top sheet

Doing this saves me so much time making my bed in the morning, and the bed always looks fresh, welcoming and neat.

I first started seeing this in European "home" magazines, when I wondered how they got their beds to look so clean and elegant. I love the simplicity of having just two rectangular pillows and one big, fluffy square duvet (comforter cover). And if I'm too busy to do my laundry, I just flip the duvet over and I get a few more days of use.

If you've shopped for sheets, you know it's quite easy to get overwhelmed. There are so many choices, and retailers most often sell their sheets in sets. That means you get two pillowcases, a top sheet and a bottom sheet. What happens if your bed has four pillows? Or you use a duvet and don't need a top sheet?

A duvet can be custom made by your local tailor, often for less money than it costs to purchase a ready-made one. Use two flat sheets sewn together. Then add a zipper, not buttons, as this will take less time to make. I think of my duvet as a sleeping bag for my down comforter.

7. Place a scented candle or a single fragrant flower on your nightstand

Just clearing away the clutter from your bedside table will show how many things you hold on to. I know people who keep unkempt piles of unread books right beside where they spend one third of their lives.

A stack of books and newspapers only reminds me of how little time I have to read, and this creates stress.

Once the books are cleared away, remove all the contraptions like *Kindles*, *Nooks*, *iPads*, mini *iPads*, headphones and laptops. Having done this, you are on your way to creating a bedside haven.

If the flower market or deli doesn't have my favorite flower—the alluringly fragrant stargazer lily—I just place a scented candle nearby. Even without lighting it, its fragrance transports me to an exotic garden.

8. Keep a journal and pen by your bed

My parents taught me to follow my dreams. I'm also very grateful to my high school English teacher, who gave us the assignment of keeping a dream journal for the entire school year.

For me, this assignment has never ended and I have boxes of journals to prove it. When I get to the last page, I've made it a tradition to re-read what I've written before I move on to a fresh new journal. This cycle of reviewing is like watching the seasons change, but over a couple of hours' time. I can look at where I've travelled, what I've learned and how I've changed. I circle entries in red ink that stand out as significant, and since I keep all these journals, when I go back through an old box I can quickly look at a year and see the highlights.

Recently, I woke up at about 3:30 am. I was unsettled and a bit anxious about a work situation. I wasn't sure what to do, so I just went back to sleep. After what must have been a few hours and as the sun was rising, I woke up and quickly recalled a dream that I had just had. In that dream, the missing steps in the work situation were revealed to me. Everything became clearer.

Dreams are oracles. If I didn't have a journal open and a pen right by my bedside, I wouldn't have been able to record my dream and, in doing so, solve my problem.

9. Review your day before going to sleep; then let it all go

I learned this one many years ago from a wise old man I shared a room with at a retreat, and I've been doing it each night since then.

This man, named Prasad, said that before he allows himself to drift off to sleep at night, he "walks" through the day he's just had—like he's writing something down on a piece of paper.

He thinks about who he encountered and how he responded. Then, he said, he asks himself how he did. Was he as kind as he could have been? Did he complete all his tasks the best he could? Is there anything he wished he could do over?

When he completes his walk, he "crumples it all up" and visualizes tossing it into a fire. Gone forever, cleared for landing—as the pilot says—and beautifully free to enter the dream world of rest and refreshment.

10. Wake up an hour early

I know that if I plan on sleeping seven to nine hours a night, I'm most likely going to average about eight.

With the ongoing regularity of eight hours of sleep a night and the better quality of sleep I get from winding down before bed, waking up an hour earlier is very doable.

I notice this most dramatically on weekends. On Sunday mornings, when most people are sleeping in, I love getting up early, maybe go to a hatha yoga class (which is usually quiet and uncrowded) and then wander around outside, doing tasks or even running an errand or two. I like being able to get my things done in an extra-relaxed manner and the spaciousness of the quiet morning sets the tone for the rest of my day.

A client of mine works full time, commutes one and a half hours to work in the morning and again on the way home. She raises two young boys and has a husband. Five days a week, this same woman manages to get to the gym at 5:30 am, works out for an hour and is back at home to wake up her children, cook them breakfast and get them off to school. She goes to bed early so she can get up early. I consider her a super woman; she considers herself lucky to be able to carve out some time for herself. I've never seen her looking tired or unhappy.

CHAPTER 2

COOKING

11. Wash your fruits and vegetables

We wash ourselves regularly and I think we should do the same with our fruits and vegetables. Who knows where they've been? When I'm unpacking my groceries, I've made it a ritual to fill a big bowl with fresh water and toss in my lemons, oranges, ginger root and anything else fresh I've bought.

Even if they look clean or have been washed before, I feel that by my washing them, I'm welcoming them into my home and kitchen.

(If you get lemons with your water when eating out, think twice about dropping them into your drink. Not everyone gives their fruit the same TLC.)

Rather than using paper towels, I place the freshly-bathed produce on my dish rack to dry. For some vegetables, like potatoes, a little scrubbing also helps remove bacteria.

Be aware, too, that some produce, like strawberries and lettuce, has to be washed and dried right before eating it in order for it to taste its best.

12. Eat seasonally

We've heard it said again and again. It's so simple and so obvious, yet we often ignore this piece of ancient wisdom.

When we eat seasonally, we eat according to the way Mother Nature wants us to eat. We select the produce She is giving us at that moment. Remembering to eat seasonally connects me with my community, since I have to locate the best growers as well as be aware of what ripens when. I've had to educate myself about my food because they don't teach this stuff in school.

Buying and eating seasonally means we buy locally.

Purchasing food locally supports small businesses and farmers.

Small business owners make up the bulk of America's work force, yet they don't receive as many tax benefits as large corporations.

If the small, family-owned grocery store down the street from my apartment in Melbourne Beach, Florida goes out of business, you can be sure that something like a "7/11" will take its place. And that's the last thing I want to see. So whenever I can, I do my grocery shopping at the family-owned market. Things may cost a few cents more, but they taste many dollars better.

13. Shop at off-hours

Because I was working from home when I started my own business, I unplugged from one of the most stressful events of every work day: rush hour. Instead, I could open my laptop or start returning calls while still in my bathrobe.

The other luxury it brought was being able to run errands and shop at off–hours. Did you know that in the late mornings and early afternoons, the grocery stores are empty?

Being able to stroll through a market, rather than rush, allowed me time to read the labels and give what I was purchasing more careful consideration. The spaciousness of shopping in an uncrowded store made these tasks enjoyable for the first time. I also became more interested in cooking.

Since then, my business has grown, and I now have an office. I commute back and forth, but the one thing I haven't changed, amidst my return to a more "regular" schedule, is the luxury of shopping at off-hours.

I also keep a list of needed household items on my kitchen countertop next to my keys. Thanks, Mom, for that one! And once a week I take this list and make my purchases—in the middle of a workday.

14. Chop and prep your food in silence

I've learned to cherish and respect my food. The more that I'm connected to my body, the more I understand that how I fuel myself is how I heal myself, too. Not heal in the sense that there is something wrong with me that needs fixing, but heal as in soothe, calm, replenish, refresh.

When I prepare my food, I do it in as quiet and relaxed a manner as I can. I find this time reflective and nourishing, and I'm certain that my state of mind goes into the food that I'm preparing.

I notice this most when I'm crazed with work and barely have the time to get home, eat and go to bed. Whenever I rush to prepare a meal, it never tastes as good as the meals I cook when I'm relaxed and peaceful.

Since the state I'm in affects the food I cook, I prefer to prepare it in a clear, orderly and quiet environment so that it, too, takes on those same nourishing qualities.

15. Sing while stirring

After I've shopped, unpacked, washed and chopped my food I feel like it's now showtime! A delicious home cooked meal is coming. As I stand over the stove, I look at my meal's combination of colors and textures, and it makes me happy to be creating something unique. There will never be a composition that looks and tastes exactly like the one I'm creating now. As I add each item, I think of it as a new character walking on stage. Sometimes it makes me want to dance, but out of practicality, I sing.

I watch the butter's shape transform in the cast iron skillet, or flick on the oven light to see if the lasagna is browning, but not too much. I keep a watchful eye on the beautiful blue flame to make sure it's at the perfect setting, and one of my favorite moments is when the spaghetti water begins to triple boil! It looks like a hot tub—for pasta, not people.

I believe that singing while stirring is an acceptable form of multi-tasking.

16. Share your tasks

As my brother says, "There's no 'I' in 'team,'" and if you share a household, there is nothing more grounding and unifying than sharing tasks and creating your meals together. So much goes into planning a meal: Creating the menu. Checking the pantry. Shopping. Carrying. Walking. Driving. Unpacking. Cleaning. Chopping. Setting the table. Serving. Cleaning up.

Have you ever noticed that people in kitchens usually look like they're having fun? There's almost always conversation, playful banter and happy smiles.

One summer, my family and I rented a lake house for the month of August. One person brought a Martha Stewart cookbook and someone else brought one by Alice Waters. It was so much fun to try out new recipes. We'd discuss what we wanted our menu to be for the next day, and then devise a plan for assembling the ingredients.

Since we were on vacation, we had the time to drive around. Finding farm stands was an adventure, not a chore.

This group activity brought purpose and joy to what would otherwise have been just a mundane daily task. We all still talk about the meals we cooked and ate that summer. Corn fritters are at the top of the list.

17. Dress up your table for one

Some of my work includes redesigning people's homes. And one thing I often notice with single or newly-single people is that they often don't really "inhabit" their spaces: cardboard boxes serve as end tables. There's no place to dine and not enough chairs.

Usually, when people call on me, it's because they're going through big life changes—the loss of a mate, a now-empty nest, or a first big salaried and important job.

But something great happens when you set up your home properly, even if it's just for you.

This same magic applies to meals. Even if we're living with someone, we still have some meals alone. Why is it okay to use nice china and real crystal when we're with others, but a plastic fork and paper plate will do when we're alone?

When I eat by myself at home, I use a cotton or linen napkin and placemat. I set my meal on a tray and I sit in a comfortable, soft dining chair in my main room, or in my favorite armchair in my bedroom. If I want real luxury, I prop myself up in bed with two pillows with a lit candle on my bedside table. I can do this for breakfast, lunch *and* dinner, depending on my schedule and my mood.

Dining this way feels like room service in some lovely hotel. When I eat alone this way, I never feel lonely.

18. Have meals with a variety of colors and textures

Good design requires editing, thoughtfulness and a sense of color, line, balance, symmetry and texture. So does good cooking.

While the cool minimalism of the late 1980's and '90's left we Americans with tuna tartare and monochromatic dressing as the cultural standard, I think we're finally swinging back to something softer and more colorful. Think of the difference between a solid color canvas and a more densely textured and colored oil painting. The colorful oil is more dynamic.

Before I eat, I look at everything on my plate. Variations in color and in texture make for a far more attractive palette. And this stimulates not only my eyes, but my stomach.

19. Eat the way your ancestors did

When I was growing up, milk was delivered to our house every few days. My mother remembers having fresh bread delivered to her doorstep. My grandmother called her refrigerator her "ice box" because that's what it originally was: a box filled with ice that kept things cool—as long, that is, as the ice lasted.

Back then, people had to think more carefully about what and when they ate. There wasn't much "convenience food," and the use of chemical fertilizers, hormones and genetic modification was unknown.

In some cities, you can now have your groceries delivered to your doorstep. Yes, that is convenient, but it can also disconnect us from our food.

While visiting my father's homeland as a child, one of my pre-dinner chores was to clean the rice and to remove the little pebbles. On one of these early trips, an auntie asked what I wanted for dinner. I said, chicken.

It wasn't until much later that I realized the chicken we'd eaten was the one I had seen earlier, wandering the yard. I'd had cage free chicken way before it was even cool!

20. Refine your palate

When the organic wave first began, I checked it out and I found that organic broccoli tasted different from the regular kind. At first I thought I was making it up, but then I started trying other types of produce and I found the same thing.

What I also realized is that my palate, or taste buds, was unaccustomed to unprocessed foods or to produce that was grown without chemicals. This, for me, was an alarming insight.

On my first trip to Italy, I noticed that the produce there seemed brighter and more beautiful. Was it simply *Bella Italia*? Maybe. But upon investigation, I learned that the bulk of the produce was locally grown, and therefore fresh and always in season.

Call it an acquired taste, but I'm so grateful that my eating habits have become more refined. I appreciate not only the taste of pure produce but I am able to enjoy single ingredient foods. This means I don't need to fuss with a lot of spices or sauces, and I can purchase my food as I need it with little or no preparation time. Think of a fresh bunch of Swiss chard chopped and sautéed with some olive oil and salt. Delicious and nutritious.

CHAPTER 3

EATING

21. Use placemats

A frame gives a photograph or a painting a context. It's a practical embellishment that elevates the viewer's attention as it protects the piece within.

Since I've taken the time to prepare a nourishing meal, I like to frame this meal and moment with a placemat, since there will never be another like it.

I used to think placemats were a clichéd, 1950's suburban novelty, but the older I get the more I see that whether I'm eating solo or with others, this decorative element enhances my experience.

Even if I buy prepared food, I take the time to remove it from its container, place it on nice china along with proper silverware and position it on a placemat.

Food is beauty, and something beautiful always quiets my mind and invites my heart.

22. Eat whatever you want on Saturdays

Growing up, I looked forward to Saturdays for one reason—the cartoons! I went to sleep on Friday night with almost the same anticipation as the night before Christmas. I was so excited to see Bugs Bunny, Scooby Doo and, later, The Three Stooges.

We all like to look forward to things. However, we only look forward to something when we don't have it all the time.

As I've said, we're humans, not machines, and flexing our different muscles is very important for our balance, health and longevity. If we perform the same exercise all the time, we can actually wear those muscles down rather than strengthening them.

Plus, doesn't it feel good to do something "bad" every now and again?

23. Don't diet

In my mind, dieting is associated with one thing only: a yo-yo. To me, it feels like a jail sentence or like being punished. I don't diet because it makes me feel contracted and claustrophobic. I much prefer a lifestyle change.

If something sounds too good to be true, it probably is. Most popular diets are sensationalized fads and don't really address each person's individual body chemistry.

A good friend of mine had terrible migraines for years and finally found relief through acupuncture and Chinese medicine. By simply adjusting his daily intake of food, he cured a crippling physical ailment.

Developing the patience to diligently alter my eating habits and to hear what my body is telling me takes both strength and simplicity.

24. Alter your lifestyle to support your well-being

Ah, gentleness, so rare and so uncommon! This I can get my head around. Gently adjusting my lifestyle means I carefully consider what I am doing and how I do it.

With this approach, I can begin to connect the dots and know what's right for me. Too much coffee makes me anxious and jittery, but I like its taste and smell. The answer? I enjoy a single cup in the morning and think twice before giving in to the craving for more.

Remember those vintage Coca-Cola bottles with their sexy curves and vibrant red logo? Now consider the size of those early bottles—small, as in 6.5 ounces small. Cola was once considered a treat to enjoy every once in a while, not something to drink daily.

Ahhhhh, moderation!

25. Light a candle at dinner

Candles are lit at churches, synagogues and temples all over the world at designated times for symbolic and holy reasons.

Why does the experience of going to a nice restaurant feel so special? Perhaps it's because, most often, the lights are dim and there are lit candles on the tables. This creates a soft, romantic environment.

Poems and songs have been written just about candles.

When I sit for dinner, I see it as a time for self-replenishment and reflection on the day, as well as a time for gratitude. This is a moment for celebration. A candle at dinner is like a birthday candle, but one you light to celebrate—or consecrate—the end of each and every day.

26. Sit while eating

Our hearts and stomachs are at the center of our bodies. When we're seated, both are supported, rested and nesting just below our upper torsos.

Food is a treasure and I want my body ready to receive this delicious gift.

Plus, didn't your Mom always say, "Don't eat while standing; it'll give you indigestion"?

You don't gas your car with its engine running. Slow down. Sit down. Eat and enjoy.

27. Say "grace"

Just pronouncing the word makes me pause. Look up its meaning and I'm certain you'll find at least one definition that makes you feel good. Grace can be said in so many ways. Some families hold hands and bow their heads while saying it in unison. Others make toasts and give a cheer.

I usually do it in one of two ways, depending on where I'm eating. If I'm out with others I place both hands on and around my plate and take one nice, slow, full breath in and then back out again. If I'm at home I close my eyes and think of all the steps the food in front of me went through to get on this plate. I also say thank you inside to the loving hands that prepared the meal. Both ways help to slow me down and remind me to see and taste the beauty in everything.

28. Look at everything on your plate before eating

I went to high school with someone who chewed each mouthful of food thirty-five times. I marveled at his focus and discipline. Even in a crowded dining hall, he literally savored every bite he ate.

Since we are visual creatures, we imbibe with our eyes as well as our mouths and stomachs. I liken this form of visual consuming to window-shopping.

Some of us can simply browse the local shops and feel satisfied. I remember this before every meal as I see the food that's set before me.

Gazing at my plate is eating. So I do this first because it's enjoyable and I do this slowly because it quiets me down and makes me aware of how precious what I'm doing is.

29. Eat less than you think you need

We've all heard that "bigger is better" and "go big or go home," so what I'm suggesting here might be considered odd, but sometimes different is the way to go.

Yes, there are children starving in Africa. There are children starving in our own hometowns. At the same time, we have an epidemic of obesity and the related illnesses of high cholesterol and diabetes.

The world can be unfair and often unbalanced. All that I really have control over is myself. Striving for a middle ground is a life-long practice, and one that I have the opportunity to work on each and every day, especially in terms of how much I choose to eat. There is no one looking over my shoulder to tell me what to eat or when to stop. This is my responsibility and mine alone.

Eating less than I think I need is a retraining of my mind that has a healthy impact on my body over time. It helps me manage my "wants" versus my "needs."

30. Don't drink water before or during a meal

In olden times, people learned to listen to their natural rhythms and cared for their bodies accordingly. I consider the time that I eat to be sacred, and I enjoy learning new ways to protect, enhance and nurture it.

For this wisdom, I have Dr. Naram, an Ayurvedic doctor, to thank. Ayurveda is an ancient system of traditional medicine which maintains that there is a digestive fire burning within us. It decreases in the cooler months and increases in the warmer ones. Drinking water while eating dampens its flame.

If you are toasting marshmallows, you wouldn't think of throwing water on the campfire. A flame is vital to the cooking process as well as to the eating process.

CHAPTER 4

DRESSING

31. Buy something new; give something old away

Can you imagine how clutter-free our lives would be if we practiced the above? The realization I had about this came from sheer necessity. My apartment is small and the bedroom has only one tiny walk-in closet. By tiny, I mean I know exactly how many pants, shirts, suits and shoes it will fit.

Ready? Twelve pairs of shoes, including sneakers and flip flops. Eight pairs of pants. Two suits. Three blazers. Six sweaters. Three hoodies. And twenty dress shirts (but only if they're on wire hangers).

Basically, I had no other option but to do this. I like having an orderly and attractive home. It just makes me feel good inside. What fits in that closet stays and what doesn't, goes.

Having this "problem" has taught me to shop with more care, and it makes my local *Goodwill* thrift shop very happy, too.

32. Lay your clothes out the night before

I work in the fashion business and the term we use for doing this is "lay downs." As a line of clothing is being "edited," the design group tests out various "looks" by laying out the garments and accessories either on a table, a rack or sometimes on an actual model.

This is a very important step in the process because once you actually see something instead of just conceptualizing it, the object being created—in this case, a wardrobe—clearly either works or it doesn't.

By doing this with your own outfits, you can easily decide whether or not they work for you. Very often, I'll have some idea of what I want to wear, and so I'll take those items from my closet and lay them on my bed. Then I go about some other business—showering, having breakfast or reading the paper.

When I return and look at the outfit again, I may see it differently and decide to change the color of the shirt or to select a different pair of socks. (I know a woman who has her own version of this. However, she doesn't lay out her clothes. She tries them on!) And if that's what you choose to do instead, make sure you have enough time—without rushing—to do it.

33. If you haven't worn something in a year, give it away

I'm sure this isn't the first time you've heard this recommendation. Like us all, I've had my own challenges in letting go of a piece of clothing. Maybe it's my optimism that a certain waist size will once again fit. Or it might be that an old piece of clothing holds so many pleasant memories and associations that, even though it's now in tatters, I don't want to make it a dust rag—yet.

This is a great exercise in letting go and, more importantly, in allowing yourself to have faith that, if you do, something better will come along.

Ten years ago, when I quit my job as a fashion executive and moved to Miami Beach, I had to sell my weekend house. This meant packing up not one residence, but two. The house was easy: the new owners bought everything right down to the forks and the towels.

The closet, though, was a challenge. Since I had a sizeable wardrobe due to the clothing allowance I'd had for years, I was stumped as to how to go about this early, midlife "downsizing."

I finally chose which pieces had real value to me and I gave the rest away. This simple exercise opened up for me a whole new life, a new home, a new career and a new way of trusting and knowing that God's grace will supply me with everything I need—and then some!

34. Buy less; have more

Purchasing "less" is an acquired taste. It's not for everyone and it's taken me until my forties to realize that I prefer having less clothes than more.

This is because by now, I've studied my tastes and I know what I look and feel good in; otherwise, it wouldn't be in my closet. I've also narrowed my palette, which means that most pieces I buy complement each other.

Black sweaters or shirts make me appear severe and less approachable. Since I want to be approachable yet I like dark clothing, I've made navy blue my color. Navy blue is elegant and refined and not as severe as black, yet still cuts a strong, graphic silhouette.

Most things look good with navy blue so by having it as my base, I can mix and match other things easily.

Another benefit of knowing my "color" is that it keeps me from buying the wrong things, thus saving me money. I really do buy less and have more.

35. Read beyond the labels

Do you know where your clothes come from? And by whom and how they're made? Sometimes this information isn't fully disclosed on a garment's label.

Labels on clothing will usually list the brand or manufacturer of the garment, its size, a care tag and a "made in" tag. One of the things some retailers are now doing is saying where the fabric is from, but not where the actual garment was produced.

This is because the fashion industry is coming more and more under scrutiny over issues such as child labor and unsafe working conditions.

There are also environmental issues. For instance, did you know that it takes 700 gallons of water to produce a single, colored cotton t-shirt? 700 gallons!

The more you know about your clothes, the better choices you can make when shopping.

36. Love your clothing

My father has clothes that have come in and out of style several times. He's able to wear the same pants, shirts and jackets for decades because of the loving care he gives them.

Even before it became politically correct to question dry cleaning's chemicals, abrasion and environmental impact, my father was suspect. He chose to limit having his clothing go through this process.

One laundering process we both cherish is having our shirts professionally laundered. This is because men's dress shirts are ironed or pressed while still wet. Forego-ing the "tumble dry" keeps your items lasting longer.

One of my clients is from England and she insists on a drying rack or drying closet rather than a tumble dry. Another client prefers to "line dry" sheets outside to get that wonderful, "April fresh" scent.

Obviously, it's not always easy or even possible to line dry, but the real point I'm making here is this: be open to more basic and less frequent laundering and drying. It saves energy and it also saves your clothes.

37. Be inspired by others, and listen to yourself

The fashion business is counting on your insecurity. It relies on huge marketing and advertising campaigns to create images that seduce us into thinking we need to buy into the lifestyle that they portray.

While some of them may be quite artistic, iconic or just plain attractive, these media blitzes can get deep inside of us and affect not only what we wear, but even how we see ourselves.

Instead, let's begin to know ourselves better by cultivating a quieter and simpler way of life. Getting rid of excess and distraction helps to open us up to seeing who and what we really are. As we do this, it becomes very natural to observe and self-select the exact style, color, trend or piece of clothing that's right for each one of us.

This is a more powerful and authentic way of both dressing and living.

38. Wash gently

When I do my laundry, my hand still goes automatically to the highest heat level or the longest dry cycle. I have to remind myself to take it easy, slow down and wash (and dry) gently and with care.

One of the more successful retail promotions of recent years was the cold wash pledge by Levi's Jeans. Upon purchasing their jeans, I was asked by the sales girl to sign a pledge card. This postcard-sized document was part of an initiative to raise awareness of the high cost of heating water and its environmental impact.

Call me gullible, but I signed the pledge and started doing my "darks" in cold water.

I wash gently and with care. For me, it's a life lesson. Take it easy on myself, take it easy on my clothes, and take it easy on my planet.

39. Shop occasionally

I've noticed I find the best pieces of clothing when traveling. Part of this has to do with having access to things that I wouldn't find at home. Another part is that I'm just more relaxed and at ease.

Since I don't shop for clothes that often, when I do, it's a treat.

I buy in five's. When I find something I like, I go for it. If I see dress shirts on sale and it's time for replacements, I'll purchase five of them—one for each work day. The result of this "bulk" shopping is that I won't have to think about buying more dress shirts for a very long time.

My buying habits are need-focused rather than consumption-driven.

40. Have a wardrobe budget

My grandmother belonged to a "travelers' club." Each week, she took a portion of her pay and put it into a bank account meant only for vacations.

This account must have had a lot of meaning to her, because I would see on her face a lovely satisfaction as she placed her weekly allotment in the deposit envelope and gave it to the teller.

Inevitably, they would have a brief conversation about how this money would be spent and where my grandmother might travel.

But her satisfaction, I think, wasn't just about being able to travel; it also came from the feeling of strength and independence that working hard to support yourself brings.

Today, I do something similar. I set aside money specifically for something that brings me real joy: nice, attractive, honestly made navy blue clothing.

CHAPTER 5

COMMUTING

41. Don't use your commute to catch up on phone calls

Sandwiching people and loved ones between work and other daily commitments is multi-tasking, and it doesn't feel good to me—or to them. If you're walking to the office and having a phone conversation at the same time, what happens to the quality of your own space and time? And what is the experience of the person on the other end of the line?

When I first caught myself doing this, I realized that I overlapped tasks in almost every area of my life.

Now, when I "check in" on the phone with someone, I make sure I'm in a relaxed environment and 100% focused on that person and on our conversation. This feels kinder and more respectful towards myself and the person with whom I'm speaking.

42. Walk (Don't run)

Anyone who lived through the 1980's knows that speed then was king—and this was way before the Internet. I grew up believing that the more I did, the more I became, and the more I became, the more I was. I derived my identity and value from what I did rather than who, what and how I am.

As I've said, by the time I was 35, I was stunned at how unhappy I was. Quitting my job at the top of my game was both frightening and lifesaving. I gave myself the gift of the time and space in which to slow down and to begin to consider what made me tick and what I really wanted. What I found I wanted was to dramatically raise the bar on how I took care of myself, and the quality of my life.

As a consequence, I feel that I have become a more "valuable" contributor to this game called life.

Now I walk, instead of running.

I make sure I have time for myself in the mornings before leaving the house. I'll sip coffee at my table or stop for breakfast on my way to work. Or I'll try to schedule meetings later in the morning—not first thing. This way I can take care of my own business before I take care of someone else's. It's that simple.

Life is a journey, not a footrace. Walk.

Why run?

43. Vary your route

Most workers commute at least 240 times a year. Add the return commute, and that's 440 commutes annually. Question: do we have to take the same route back and forth every day?

Constantly working the same muscle is non-productive; even an all-star basketball player will incorporate other exercises like swimming or *Pilates*. Sports trainers say this variety of movement helps create balance within the body and enhances the player's ultimate performance.

I like broccoli; I don't eat it every day.

I can walk or take a subway, a bus or a car from my home to my office. Walking is my number one choice because it clears my head. It's also very healthy: it moves the lymph throughout my body. And I like to take different routes; sometimes, I let the traffic lights determine my course.

And unless it's oppressively humid and hot, I always walk on the sunny side of the street. Literally.

44. Listen to music

Nothing reminds me of my glorious teenage years more than driving around with loud music playing. And I still do it to this day. Not all the time, surely, and not in quiet neighborhoods, but definitely on the open highway.

Nothing shifts my mood more quickly than listening to music. If I'm on a bus or a subway, I turn up the volume, and then when I'm back out on the street, I turn it back down so I can be aware of any potential hazards.

It's like having a secret: no one but me knows what I'm hearing as I escape into my own inner disco.

45. Watch the road

Once I was driving with a good friend. He looked up and said, "See all those cars? Each one is driven by an individual mind. See the way each car moves differently from side to side? If there weren't yellow lines on the road, they'd be all over the place."

I use the time while driving to watch my mind, even as I watch the road. It's always interesting to see where my mind goes when I give it its space and freedom.

I remember a question on my driving test: "Is it okay while driving to allow your eyes to move around, or should you instead stare straight ahead?" The correct answer was: "Allow your eyes to scan the road and roadside so you can be more aware of potential hazards."

46. Read books, not your emails

When I'm in transit, I like to stay focused on getting to my destination safely and on time. This means I've already done all my prep work for the meeting or occasion. Doing so frees up my time and space during the journey. Whether it's a ten-minute subway ride or two hours on a bus, I enjoy this downtime.

I keep some of my favorite books on my phone so I can enjoy a good read wherever I am. I don't like to read or answer my emails while travelling because I know that the quality of my attention isn't as strong as when I do it seated quietly at my desk.

47. Know where you're going

Make a note of the address you're going to and bring it along with you.

It will remind you where you're headed and can be especially helpful if you get lost.

This tip comes from years of my own traveling on business and finding myself in some dicey situations. It's a muscle I've strengthened and now know that I have.

Today, I can end up anywhere in the world and still figure out how to get from point A to point B.

The trick is to be prepared and to do your research beforehand, not while travelling—or when you're lost!

48. Arrive early

I'd rather arrive early than late. It allows me the space to settle in before beginning whatever I'm there to do. The result is my feeling more relaxed and better able to give a full 100% to the task at hand.

In A.A., they suggest the same thing to their members. Leave early, arrive early. Give yourself plenty of time. The pressure of being late is a well-known trigger for a relapse into drinking.

Perhaps if I lived south of the border or worked in a slower paced job or environment, I'd operate differently— but probably not. I prefer to live my life in a calm and ordered fashion, and this discipline assists me in offering my best to any and all of life's situations.

49. Go for a dry run

My father often performs a dry run or "dress rehearsal" for anything that involves a car trip to an unfamiliar destination. If he has an appointment tomorrow in a part of town where he hasn't ever been, he'll head out today to locate the address.

Before any journey, an open road atlas will become the focus of his attention for days before. It's the logical yet magical way that he orients himself to his future surroundings.

Planning something is often as exciting, if not more, than actually doing that thing. Why do you think people window shop?

50. There's no place like home

A television commercial from some years ago had a woman proclaim, "I run home from work just as fast as I do getting there." I feel the same way, except I don't run.

I was born at home. My father, a doctor, delivered me; my brother was there and, obviously, so was my mother. This relatively unique event imprinted and impacted how I feel about my home and fuels a natural desire to remain close to my family. I love my home. And I enjoy completing my business tasks so I can return to its softer, gentler surroundings.

Home is where my heart is. It's a state of mind and it's a physical place, too.

When the pendulum swings one way I go to work, and when it reverses, I go home. Strength. Simplicity.

CHAPTER 6

WORKING

51. Give a theme to each work day

Discipline gives me focus, and focus gives me balance. Having a gentle discipline frames both me and my day. This gentle structure holds me up in the same way I imagine my bones supporting my body and its movements.

For instance, take exercise: I feel better when I do it, so I want to do it daily. Thus, my intention is to work out every day. Obviously, things come up, schedules shift, meeting times and project tasks change, but in the back of my head and on my calendar I plan the form of exercise I'm going to do each day: usually hatha yoga one day and spinning class the next. This creates a pattern that supports my staying in shape and being physically fit. And it's as simple as marking down the time of each exercise class on my calendar.

And I've begun to apply daily themes to my work. I find this very helpful in keeping both myself and my team focused and organized. Monday's theme is PLANNING—for the week ahead. Tuesday's is SHOPPING—for anything that's needed in the studio or for a client. Wednesdays are for BILLING—we collect, document and submit anything related to payments. Thursdays are for FILING—any paperwork randomly lying around gets filed correctly. And Fridays are for CLEANING—all surfaces get wiped: desktops, tables, chairs, window sills, blinds, computers and floor.

That way, my creativity is free to play.

52. Rethink your career every twelve months

We regularly reboot our computers and mobile devices. If my *iPhone* is acting strangely, I power it down and then turn it back on. Everything and everybody needs to turn off now and again by sleeping, dreaming or taking a vacation. In a world that changes faster than we can comprehend, how can we not regularly dedicate some time to relooking at how we earn our living, as well?

For my entire adult life, I've used the time between Christmas and New Year's to think about what I want from the year to come. I like this time because most people are preoccupied with the holidays and travelling to visit friends and family and so my work life is quieter.

It's not that I don't visit family myself or enjoy the season's excitement, but I also use this time to pull back into myself and get a fresh perspective.

If a retreat or vacation isn't possible then, I'll dedicate an afternoon to sitting on my sofa or taking a long walk in the park. Before I start out, I ask the deepest part of myself for direction, praying, "Tell me what I need to know in order to become closer to you."

This tip isn't new. An old Sufi poet put it like this:

> *Now the New Year reviving old desires,*
> *The thoughtful soul to Solitude retires...*

53. Don't complain

When I was a boy, my next-door neighbor would always say, "I hate cutting the grass every week because it just grows back the following one." Even at the age of ten, I knew there was something wrong with his perspective. He was complaining about the inevitable—in this case, the fact that the green grass grows!

Most people are unhappy with the work they do. Complaining is so common in the workplace, it's almost become expected. Complaints have become a part of our culture and this makes me sad. I'm not saying that every moment needs to be sugar-coated, but if we begin to listen more deeply to ourselves before we start to complain, we can change both the atmosphere around us as well as our own point of view.

Most of the time I feel lucky to have a job, to earn my own money and to be able to live independently. I can't walk past someone with a guide dog or in a wheelchair without thanking my lucky stars that I see and move the way I do.

Pythagoras said: "If the wind blows ... adore the sound."

Someone else said: "Go ahead and argue with reality. But just remember, reality always wins."

54. Do what you say you'll do

Before starting my own business, I worked for a number of companies. One thing I noticed is that there was always some individual or team with a million great ideas. We could do this! We could build that! Their vision and enthusiasm was always exciting, except that it was often little more than just talk.

In those days, I was more reserved. At meetings, I would listen to everyone's ideas and when the meeting was over, digest what I'd heard. When showtime came and we had to produce, I noticed that often it was the person or team with the million ideas that was no closer to making any of them happen.

Slowly, I began to offer my own suggestions and, on projects I proposed, I had some measure of success. When I look back at this time, I know this success came from my being accountable to my word. I became someone who delivered what he had promised. I did what I said I would.

This matters.

55. Get up every hour and move

Anyone who's seen that famous scene from the 1950's comedy television show "I Love Lucy"—the one with Lucy and Ethel working on an assembly line in a chocolate factory—knows about the trouble that can arise from monotony.

Why this hilarious episode is so funny is because it reveals something about our nature. Lucy and Ethel's job is to stand in place all day and wrap chocolates as they move past them on an assembly line. It demonstrates how we can't do the same thing over and over and over again without getting bored or overwhelmed, and then making mistakes.

For me, this symbolizes the fast pace of our modern post-industrial life and the futility of even trying to keep up with it. Even Lucy says, "I think we're fighting a losing game."

It doesn't feel good to sit or stand in one place, one way, for too long. Think about taking a bus or plane trip—how does your body feel after even a couple of hours?

So get up and move around. Get the breath going. Shake it off.

By the way, did you know that the fastest way to change your mental state is to move and change the position of your body?

56. Place a small piece of black tourmaline on your desk

I went to my acupuncturist, complaining of fatigue and queasiness. She performed all the usual tests. Then she asked if I had anything "blocking" me from my computer. I said, "Blocking? Huh?"

I'd told her I was working long hours at my computer, and she said that the electromagnetic energy coming from it was affecting my body. I'd heard about the stress that's related to the radiation emitted from devices like cell phone towers and even Wi-Fi, but had never given it much more thought—other than not using a microwave oven.

After my own research, I learned that almost everything emits an EMF (electromagnetic frequency). The EMFs from x-ray machines and from computers impact our subtle energy field and can deplete and drain our energy.

As to my acupuncturist's suggestion, which I'm passing on? I place a small piece of black tourmaline, which costs about five dollars, on my desk between me and my computer. The rock absorbs the EMFs, which allows me to write at my desk longer than I would have been able to without it, and I don't feel queasy anymore.

A placebo? Perhaps. Yet becoming more aware of my state reminds me that I have to protect, nourish and care for it. Plus, the tourmaline is beautiful, and both my office and I want all the beauty we can get.

57. Create a separate file for each project

I learned this one from Calvin Klein. In his offices, every project had a black binder with a *P-Touch* label stating its name. Whenever we got a new project, a binder was created that housed all its relevant documents, as well as an overview and contacts page. It was impressive to see all of our projects organized in such a clean and simple way.

Today, in my own business, I use the same system. Every budding project gets a clear folder with a yellow *Post-it* note on the top right-hand corner, with the project name or task handwritten with a black *Sharpie*. Once the project becomes official, it gets a black binder and a *P-Touch* label.

The one modern update is that I now also have each project folder and its info in digital format and stored on a shared drive, so that it's accessible from anywhere to anyone I want to view it.

Old school? Meet new school.

58. Make a to-do list for the next day

In my office, we take old paper and cut it into quarters to use as scrap. I put a little pile on every desk and keep one at home in my bedside drawer.

These little rectangles are a simple way for me to remind myself about what I need to do. I use *iCal* on my computer religiously to track my time with clients as well as my appointments, but I still love these little pieces of paper. Handwriting—how charming. How quaint!

When I'm winding down for the day, I take one out and write the following day's name upon it, then make a list of tasks. This helps me begin to empty my head without the fear of forgetting, and lets me leave my job at the office.

59. Make a list and check it twice, like Santa

Did you know that checking something off a list creates excitement, and that excitement creates and is created by endorphins? Some people take medication to increase their endorphins. You can also increase them by regular exercise. All physical action—even a forced smile—creates endorphins.

Try it and see; make a mental check mark next to the following:

I woke up today and was able to get out of bed.

I didn't get a speeding ticket on my way to work.

The bank teller complimented me on my shirt.

I balanced my checkbook.

I went to the gym.

Now, don't you feel better?

60. Don't try so hard

A teacher at my high school often declared, "Work hard and play hard." He also loathed a "smiley face" or the greeting, "Have a nice day." Thankfully, I've also had teachers who extol excellence over rigid perfectionism.

When I take a moment to reflect on things, I'm reminded that those things I love the most—my family, friends and home, my talents, my spiritual practices, the beauty of this life and world—are not the result of gritting my teeth and clawing my way in order to get them. They just came to me, easily.

Think about what you most cherish in your own life. Isn't it true?

I'm just grateful to be able to do something I love. Yes, I have the tendency to work hard, but fortunately I have learned a lovely new skill called gentleness.

CHAPTER 7

FRIEND-ING

61. Move closer to good friends.

A good friend is a treasure. When I leave a good friend, I feel uplifted, acknowledged and energized. I find myself smiling. I can't wait to see them again. In fact, if I'm having trouble falling asleep, I count friends, not sheep.

I nurture these relationships the way I would nurture a garden. I care for these people and that, to me, means spending time with them.

Since I value my time the way I value my money, I regularly evaluate how I spend it and with whom.

Good friends keep me anchored. They mean the world to me. I won't just give them the shirt off my back, I'll give them my whole wardrobe, small and select though it may be.

62. Edit

Decluttering other people's surroundings is something I do as part of my job. It's called editing, and every physical creation must go through this process on its way to completion. For a composition to be compelling, there needs to be dynamism. All the pieces have to work together and feel right.

Have you noticed how, at some points in relationships, things just don't fit anymore? I find that watching my various circles of friendships ebb and flow like the ocean's waves hitting a beach allows me to have a thoughtful appreciation of who is nearest to me, as well as a certain detachment from those who might have drifted away. This way, I'm able to keep positive influences close by and allow anything else to move a few paces back.

I would never ask a wave to stop and not move, and this reminds me to allow whatever comes to come, and whatever goes, to go.

63. Just say, "No"

I once had a friend, Peter. If you asked Peter to do something for you and he didn't want to, he'd say, "No." He wouldn't follow up his "no" with any explanation. He wouldn't say, "I'd love to, but I'm booked." Or, "I'm sorry" or "I wish I could." He'd just say, "No." Period. End of conversation. And there was nothing you could do but accept his answer, since he left you no room to manipulate or maneuver in. And guess what? I respected him for it all the more.

I say "yes" to life, but sometimes I have to say "no" to friends. I'm gregarious *and* I'm reflective. Listening to myself closely helps me maintain balance. Loving myself helps me to say "no" sometimes.

64. Go out

Have you ever gone to work out, then come home and said: "Gee, I wish I hadn't gone to the gym"? No. And this is because getting your blood moving and your heart rate up feels great.

I feel the same way about dancing, going out to a party with friends or going to a movie.

Even if it wasn't the best movie ever, I can always find some merit in the experience—whether it's good costumes, fun music, or a touching storyline.

Going out is enlivening since I don't do it all the time.

It's a contrast to my regular daily life.

A special event.

65. Make new friends

When I think about how many people I encounter in the course of a day, the number is staggering—store clerk, dry cleaner, doormen, clients, students, friends, friends of friends, colleagues and strangers.

Though I cherish my time alone, I know I am also emotionally fed by being with people. I learn about myself when I'm with others. I'm always amazed by the types of people I attract and mystified by why I don't attract certain others.

I consider every new person that I meet to be a potential friend. I see each one as a reflection of a part of me.

66. Get to know people

I'm a friendly person, but I take my time getting to know people. When I purchase something I enjoy learning more about it, whether it's a car, a new pair of sneakers, workout gear or a vacation destination.

It's so easy to research things online. I never stay at a hotel without reading the reviews on "Trip Advisor" and having a look at the photographs of the venues, taken by paying guests.

With people, it's a little different. Technology brings us up close and personal very quickly—often, too fast for me. As I've told you, when I find an outfit I like, I stick with it. I take time and careful consideration in selecting it and I tend to keep my clothing for some time.

That goes double for a good friend.

67. Listen

People like to talk about themselves. It's natural. I think one of the reasons I get along with most people is that I take the time to listen to them. I like listening. I learned this from my father. He takes everything in, doesn't speak unnecessarily or at great length, but he references things from last month or years ago that let me know I've been truly heard.

There is something deeply satisfying about being heard. I think it's fundamental to our happiness and it's something I enjoy doing for others.

Then again, for some people, the opposite of talking isn't listening, but waiting to talk!

Slowing down enough to really listen takes strength and simplicity—whether listening to yourself or to another.

68. Leave before the party's over

Staying past my welcome feels desperate and greedy. Every second of the day or night has a beat like a drum. Skipping or missing a beat can result in a misstep, stumble or fall. Ask any ballerina or football player.

When I listen to myself, I am better able to direct my steps, thoughts and actions. I'm more in tune with my time and environment. I know when to come and when to go.

At the end of the night, the bartender yells, "Last call!" Look around the barroom then. Is that really the crowd you want to be a part of?

69. Ask yourself questions

When I am planning or encountering a social situation, the first thing I do is ask myself if it's something I really want to do.

This is an exercise in knowing myself. Checking in. How am I feeling in this moment? Am I feeling silly and talkative? Am I feeling contemplative and inward? Is my energy high or low? Do I feel like eating or like drinking? Am I up for a one-on-one conversation, or would I prefer light chatter?

Taking this step of introspection and thoughtfulness helps me set parameters for how I want to spend my time, and it creates opportunities for me to invent possibilities that I would otherwise not have considered.

70. Stay connected

If you have a friend who, even if you haven't seen them in years, you can start right up with as if you had just been with them, you are one lucky person. This level of connection is very rare.

After I've spent time with a friend, I'll usually follow up the next day with a quick text or email to say, "That was fun" or "Great seeing you" or "Thank you for meeting me for dinner last night."

How and why we meet and befriend someone is mystifying, isn't it? Yet staying connected to people is like tending a garden. Cultivating the soil. Watering the seeds. Watching the plants grow and change.

I love keeping in touch with my friends, because I love them. It's that simple.

CHAPTER 8

DECORATING

71. Move things around before buying something new

A painting starts with a blank canvas. Ideally, so does decorating. But how realistic is this, unless you've just lost everything or are moving out of your parents' home and don't have any furniture at all?

Most of us have lots of "stuff." Furniture, equipment, objects d'art and memorabilia—things we cherish. So when the time comes to redecorate, begin by taking your existing possessions into careful consideration. Some might go and some might stay.

But how do you know which ones?

First, move things around. A new seating arrangement may be enough to make the room feel warmer and more inviting. Maybe changing the lighting will make the room more user-friendly.

Do this first before buying anything new. Your ideal interior may be there right in front of you, just waiting to be revealed.

72. Think like a film director

For a number of years, I worked for the iconic fashion designer, Ralph Lauren. I knew I wanted to work with him from the very first time I passed his store—the Rhinelander Mansion—on Madison Avenue.

When it opened in 1986, it was revolutionary both in scale and in its richness of materials and finishes. Entering it was like walking into a scene from F. Scott Fitzgerald's "The Great Gatsby." From its limestone façade to its brass door handles to the aged Persian carpet runners, the place exuded an opulence and luxury that felt almost otherworldly.

Its maintenance and attention to detail was not unlike that given to a museum's galleries. One thing I learned while working there was that Ralph once dreamt of directing movies.

To me, this made perfect sense since film directors—and their large teams of costume, set and production designers—create virtual worlds to support the storyline of a film.

Now, imagine you are the (art) director of your home, the film director of your life. Cup your hand and place it over one eye. Survey your space and ask yourself, "Is this the best set for the movies of my life, the ideal backdrop for my dreams?"

And, if it isn't, then why not change it?

73. Begin from within

Usually a decorator walks in and says, "New sofa, new drapes, paint the walls, move the carpet, and for heaven's sake, let's get rid of those end tables—ugh!—and we'll find you some better art work! Ok?"

But decorating my way means changing your life: start from the inside out and begin by building a firm foundation.

I worked with an architect well-known for his signature minimalism—cool limestone floors, stark white walls and rooms with a single chair or table. The look is arresting and, at first, quite calming, but no one actually lives like that! In his own home, behind beautifully-hinged sliding doors, was a space for his kids, filled with toys, books, soft carpets and colorfully made beds.

There is nothing wrong with "stuff." But no amount of stuff will ever make up for that which you feel you do not have.

At the same time, what you possess and display in your home should flow from a real, living need and be an expression of your dreams and nature. Otherwise, it might be nice in a magazine, or even to visit, but who'd want to live there?

74. Paint, if you can't redecorate

Once, only the wealthy hired interior designers. Now, transforming your home by redecorating it is on any one of the many channels or shows dedicated to home design. Decorating has become mainstream, and with that change has come an overwhelming amount of information and design choices.

An interior designer can and should save his or her client money by helping the client make smarter choices, as well as avoid costly mistakes, like buying a sofa that won't fit through the door.

Yet if you don't have the resources to hire a professional to redesign your home, do this: go to a paint store and select three color swatches—no more! Look at their colors in your home's morning, afternoon and evening light. Sleep on your decision. Then choose the color that looks the best.

Painting means moving everything out of the room or into its center. This is a great opportunity for a deep clean. This natural and practical step will leave your room refreshed, with a new tone and a sparkle that only a good cleaning can offer.

75. Have a clear vision

If two people are over affectionate in public, a passerby might say:"Hey, get a room!" Everything has a time and a place and the same holds true for decorating.

"Getting a room" to me means having a vision—of who you are and what you love.

Start by envisioning the end result, the goal. Create in your mind a room or space that transports you to another, better world. By this, I mean an artfully appointed dwelling that suits you and the way you wish to live: well.

Some of the ways you can find inspiration are:

Looking at images in magazines;

Photographing rooms, lobbies, bathrooms, stores and hotels when traveling;

Viewing blogs like *Instagram*, *Houzz*, *Tumblr*, *Remodelista*, *Boom*… and *Pinterest*.

And my personal favorite:

Sitting in the room you want to change, closing your eyes and asking the room itself to tell you how it wants to look and be.

76. Love twos

Balance is harmony and for there to be harmony, there has to be two. And who doesn't want a harmonious home?

This is one reason we see twos everywhere: two cement lions in front of a restaurant; two hand-blown glass hurricane lamps on either end of a fireplace mantel in a lakeside cabin; two sofas flanking a large window at a beach house; two foo dogs at the entrance to a large office building in Hong Kong.

Are you single and would like to find a mate? Make sure you have a double bed with two bedside tables, not just one. And keep your room open and free of clutter so your new love will have plenty of space.

77. Love threes

You've heard the expression: "The third time's the charm." Objects in threes make a more interesting composition, and the roots of a trinity are indeed holy:

- Jesus, Mary and Joseph

- Father, Son and Holy Spirit

- Alpha, Omega and Infinity

- The great Pyramids of Cairo in Egypt

When I was young, I used to ask my Mom why she displayed objects in sets of three around the house—on living room side tables, on the bathroom counters and even on the wall.

Her response was, "It just looks better that way." It's true and it's funny… and I feel the same way.

78. Bring outdoor fabric in

For a time, it seemed, all my clients were the parents of young children. Designing an attractive space and factoring in all the little spills and the hand- and footprints made by their children and pets used to be a challenge—hence, the hideous plastic coverings over sofas and chairs in the 1950's and the formal, though rarely if ever used, living rooms.

Whenever I suggest using outdoor fabrics for indoor furniture, my clients sometimes think I'm recommending those thick, stiff fabrics that came in weak, sun bleached colors. But outdoor fabrics aren't like that anymore. They've been amazingly re-purposed and reinvented; so much so, that I almost prefer them, with or without kids.

Today's outdoor fabrics are made up of tiny, hollow, acrylic spaghetti. These hollow channels are then injected with color.

Try this: buy a bolt or a few yards of this kind of fabric and put it in your washing machine and dryer. It will come out looking and feeling like your softest, favorite pair of khakis. Most people will swear they are sitting on 100% cotton! Except that spilled ink, blood, wine, mud and marinara sauce wipe right off.

79. Return to the classics

I was always a fan of the writer, Henry David Thoreau. I marvel how, in the 1800's, he was already concerned about the complexities of "modern" life and chose to move to the woods on the outskirts of town. There, on Walden Pond, he built himself a one room cabin. Having the strength to change one's life and environment is to me one very real definition of courage.

And thanks to another great American writer and poet, Ralph Waldo Emerson, author of "Self-Reliance," I know that the strength and the courage we need are there; that vast inner resources are ours for the asking when we stand in the light of our own true beliefs and try our best to live by them.

I feel the same way about designing. I rely upon the timeless power of the classics. I prefer solid, well-made things over ones that are trendy. Designs long used are not only deeply embedded in our psyche, but are with us still because they're trusted, work and provide enduring value.

80. Change is good

I had a boss once who walked around saying, "Change is good." At that time—almost 20 years ago—I would roll my eyes and think to myself, No thanks. I'd rather not change.

As the years went by and I began to recount the steps I have taken to create the life I have now, I see that I've learned to embrace change and have actually come to thrive on it.

Your home is your reflection. If you want a better image, then change it.

Moving things around your home creates change.

CHAPTER 9

RESTING

81. Turn off the television

I like TV. I sometimes enjoy watching a morning program while getting ready for work, or I'll spend a Sunday afternoon watching a classic movie. I think of TV in the same way I think of dessert and Coca-Cola: a little of it goes a long way.

For me, TV is activating and numbing simultaneously. Activating in that it stimulates my senses, but numbing in that there is a constant stream of non-essential information hosing down my brain.

Therefore, I try to make sure there's a good reason for turning it on. Is it because I'm resting? Or because I'm avoiding something?

82. Silence your cell phone

Why do some people use loud ringers on their mobile phones? You know the kind, the ones that make everyone in the restaurant stop eating and turn around.

We live in an age where almost everyone has a mobile phone, meaning we are no longer ever incommunicado. We almost always have our phones with us—even in the bathroom! Since we now seem to have this constant companion, it's a good idea to lay down some ground rules on how we can best coexist.

My number one rule is: Keep your phone's ringer on silent-flash or silent-vibrate. Number two: At night, put the phone on regular ring and set it on the other side of your bedroom.

It's so easy, so simple: silent-flash or silent-vibrate. Quieting my outer environment quiets my inner one, too.

83. Want to be alone

One of the biggest challenges in an age of constant accessibility is figuring out how much or how little of it is right for you. For me, the amount often changes and so I monitor it regularly. I do this because, when I'm over-scheduled, my body becomes jerky and my digestion, sluggish.

When this happens, I know it's time to scale back on my interactions and do something that quiets me down.

Sometimes, being quiet allows me to observe parts of myself that I would otherwise not see. This can be confronting and uncomfortable.

Yet by allowing myself to travel through this discomfort, I inevitably emerge feeling brighter and stronger.

84. Stare at the horizon

I once went to my trusted chiropractor, complaining of fatigue and eyestrain. This was before the Internet and at a time when the only computer I used was the one at work. After carefully scanning and testing my body, he offered some advice I have used ever since:

"Walk down to the river and look out at the horizon."

My eyes, he said, were only focusing on what was up close and right in front of me and, consequently, my body and mind followed my eyes.

This is also an old mariner's trick to avoid motion sickness while on choppy waters.

85. Take short rests throughout your day

I'm not recommending you sleep or lounge around all day, although either one may be necessary and enjoyable from time to time. It's taking brief rests that allows you to maintain your poise and focus for long periods of time. Many successful and busy people know this.

The trick is to find short rest periods even in the midst of working: a long pause while giving a presentation, a slightly slower pace while jogging or even a glance out the window into the far distance every now and then. This brief pause during regular activity can replenish and refresh us.

Years ago, I asked a monk where the rivers of joy and sorrow meet. He said, "In the space between the breaths."

I don't experience the fatigue I used to, and I owe it in large part to watching my breath coming in and going out as often as I can.

Why don't you try it?

86. Treat your time as money

When I began working for myself, one of the biggest lessons I learned was this: my time is money!

Switching to a fee-for-services model meant that I was "renting myself out" for allotted periods, during which I performed specific services. In other words, when I'm working, I get paid for every minute and when I'm not, I'm earning zip.

At first, I felt the need to work 100% of the time—morning, noon and night. I was constantly sprinting to keep up. Later, I scaled back to more "regular hours," changing my pace to a brisk jog or walk. Today, I feel more like I'm surfing and I can enjoy the ebb and flow of my business and life.

The biggest lesson I've learned is to truly value my time, because myself and my time have incalculable worth and value.

87. Walk slowly

One thing I need to remind myself of almost every day is to walk more slowly.

Just because I'm in a competitive environment doesn't mean that I have to rush around competitively. Especially on my very active days, I use the time while walking to slow down and to steady my mind.

Walking down a hallway or up the street for an appointment, I purposely slow it down. I correct my posture, make sure my shoulders are down and not up near my ears and that my chin is tucked in. This gives my neck a lot more room and just by doing this subtle adjustment, I look—and feel—two inches taller!

88. Cherish contrast

We all long for contrast.

When my parents plan a vacation, they often go to an urban environment. Since they live on the beach, the excitement of a trip to a city is stimulating and refreshing because it's something different.

Conversely, since I live and work in a densely populated city, when I look for destinations to travel to I invariably go for the deserted beach or isolated mountain retreat.

This is a wonderful thing to do.

Contrast is one of the qualities that makes a painting, a photograph—and often a life—beautiful.

89. Put your feet up

I heard this once, though I'm not sure from where or whom:

"Why run if you can walk?"

"Why walk if you can sit?"

"Why sit if you can lounge?"

As you already know, I'm not a big lounger—except when it's well-deserved.

So when I do sit down and put my feet up, it makes me feel like I'm on vacation. The engine is off and I am at rest.

It's a great "exercise," when used in moderation!

90. Go more slowly

A friend's mother was famous for saying, "If you think you're going slow, go slower."

Even repeating this sentence aloud makes me slow down.

If

You

Think

You're

Going

Slooow,

Go

Slooooower.

CHAPTER 10

THINKING

91. Take time to ground yourself

On Mondays, my head is often unusually clear. Why? Because I've taken Saturday and Sunday off. On Saturdays, I savor and delight in the space of the weekend: sleeping in, then maybe getting together with friends or family. In short, playing.

When I do this, I feel content and when Sunday comes, I'm so grateful for another day off that I treat each minute as if it's gold. This is a stimulating and rewarding practice. It quiets and grounds me.

Once I'm grounded, I'm better able to choose and edit my thoughts, as well as to tackle the week ahead.

92. Write it down

Albert Einstein never remembered telephone numbers. He believed it was a waste of his brain power to retain information that could just as easily be looked up.

The brain is mysterious. It has such strength and power, like a raging river. I think of its "raging" as an aspect of its creativity. Always moving. Always flowing. Always creating, even when I'm asleep and dreaming.

I'm a creative person, working in a creative field. My task is to come up with fresh ideas and make them real. In order to not feel overwhelmed, I take lots of notes. I know I have to write things down—especially my inspirations—or else I will lose them.

If I lose them, then they don't become realized. They just float away. Writing them down is a way for me to capture the creativity coming through me and harness and retain it for future use.

I keep a day journal, a dream journal and a money journal. I write notes to myself constantly, including lists of what I need to do. These are my love notes to myself.

93. Drive

The joy and freedom of the open road is epitomized in the movie, "Easy Rider." A great feeling of joy comes to me when I'm driving on an open highway—even if it's not on a motorcycle.

Since I live in the city, I don't need to own a car. So when I need to, I rent one and it feels like pure escape. It's so liberating to just get away. Even if I'm on my way to work, I can still use the drive to be with myself. I find this incredibly recharging.

94. Regularly hit the stop button

It's a balancing act: removing one's self from one's daily activities, schedules, duties and obligations in order to become refreshed and refocused. Yet getting away from something for a while yields the opportunity to return with a new perspective.

The analogy I like to use is taking the bus home at night. A few blocks before my stop, I have to hit the stop button in order to signal the driver that I want to get off at the next one.

And if I don't hit that button, I'll surely miss my stop.

95. Think before acting

Of all the means I use to live a balanced life, this is the one I have the biggest problem doing. I'm not sure if it's because I like moving and acting quickly or that it's just a very old, deeply ingrained habit.

I know that when I do take an extra moment to pause and consider what I'm about to say or do, what I say or do is usually better.

The visual I use to remind myself of this is watching the cliff divers in Acapulco. They don't run to the edge of the cliff and jump! They walk slowly and solemnly up to the edge. They pause to gauge the tide and depth of the water below, assuring themselves first that they can dive safely.

Only then do they draw a deep breath, outstretch their arms, lower their knees and spring forward.

96. Contemplate

I used to criticize myself for being in therapy. For years I felt I was wasting my time and money. It felt indulgent—almost a Woody Allen, New York City cliché—to dedicate time, energy and money to discussing what went on in my head.

I often thought I should be doing something more important. It was many years later, post-therapy, when I read that contemplation is a highly revered spiritual practice.

Voila! Just reading those words changed how I perceived the time I'd spent thinking things through. It helped me get clear on what I wanted and now, I live the life of my dreams. By that I mean, a life made up of consideration for myself and for others, combined with a deep love for this world.

What could be more "spiritual" than loving and caring for one's own self?

97. Explore your options, then choose

There are a million routes that lead from point A to point B. For me, exploring the route is the start of any journey. It's both grounding and exciting to know where you'd like to go, to think things through, then choose your route and take that first step forward.

Stepping back and looking at things from every angle before you proceed is a useful way of studying one's self, as well.

98. Relish early Sunday mornings

While I don't go to church, I still consider Sunday holy. Practicing meditation daily since my early twenties affords me the opportunity to pray often—and any and everywhere.

One of my favorite painters is Edward Hopper, whose depictions of mundane urban life tell wonderfully quiet and reflective stories. Perhaps the best example of this is the masterpiece, "Early Sunday Morning, 1930." There's not a single Sunday morning in New York that I don't see his image of a deserted street, with the sunrise reflected in the rich red bricks of lower Seventh Avenue.

Time is marked by those events that we consider important. I consider Sunday important because it's when I can take a break from routine and swim in more placid waters. This clears my head and gets me ready for the week ahead.

99. Go ahead: decide

When I was younger, it seemed that I could never make up my mind. I would just stay undecided forever.

Now that I'm running my own business, I don't have that luxury. I'm paid to problem-solve. And if I don't provide solutions, I'm not doing my job.

Perfectionism can be crippling. You're unable to make decisions and to move forward in your life.

This perfectionism can disguise itself in many forms: lethargy, procrastination, anxiety, even depression. I've been there and I won't go back.

For me, the "80/20" principle works magic. I aim for making something correct, attractive and practical, and I'm okay with getting it 80% right rather than 100%. That way, things get decided, finished, done.

100. Have fun

Abraham Lincoln said: "People are as happy as they make up their minds to be."

Every moment I have that decision to make: whether or not to be happy and to enjoy my life.

Having fun is the "icing on the cake." The daily personal rituals I've shared with you here enhance every moment of my life. They are the steady ticking of my clock: strength and simplicity.

They offer me comfort and they cost me nothing. They keep me safe but not separate, connecting me more closely to my world and myself.

And after work and contemplation, celebration.

After fasting, feasting.

STRENGTH

SIMPLICITY

100 WAYS

1. Press your pillowcases
2. Start winding down about two hours before sleep
3. Have a beautiful image within sight of your bed
4. Sleep seven to nine hours
5. Use a traditional alarm clock
6. Use a duvet with no top sheet
7. Place a scented candle or a single fragrant flower on your nightstand
8. Keep a journal and pen by your bed
9. Review your day before going to sleep; then let it all go
10. Wake up an hour early
11. Wash your fruits and vegetables
12. Eat seasonally
13. Shop at off-hours
14. Chop and prep your food in silence
15. Sing while stirring
16. Share your tasks
17. Dress up your table for one
18. Have meals with a variety of colors and textures
19. Eat the way your ancestors did
20. Refine your palate
21. Use placemats
22. Eat whatever you want on Saturdays
23. Don't diet

24. Alter your lifestyle to support your well-being

25. Light a candle at dinner

26. Sit while eating

27. Say "grace"

28. Look at everything on your plate before eating

29. Eat less than you think you need

30. Don't drink water before or during a meal

31. Buy something new; give something old away

32. Lay your clothes out the night before

33. If you haven't worn something in a year, give it away

34. Buy less; have more

35. Read beyond the labels

36. Love your clothing

37. Be inspired by others, and listen to yourself

38. Wash gently

39. Shop occasionally

40. Have a wardrobe budget

41. Don't use your commute to catch up on phone calls

42. Walk (Don't run)

43. Vary your route

44. Listen to music

45. Watch the road

46. Read books, not your emails

47. Know where you're going

48. Arrive early

49. Go for a dry run

50. There's no place like home

51. Give a theme to each work day

52. Rethink your career every twelve months

53. Don't complain

54. Do what you say you'll do

55. Get up every hour and move

56. Place a small piece of black tourmaline on your desk

57. Create a separate file for each project

58. Make a to-do list for the next day

59. Make a list and check it twice, like Santa

60. Don't try so hard

61. Move closer to good friends

62. Edit

63. Just say, "No"

64. Go out

65. Make new friends

66. Get to know people

67. Listen

68. Leave before the party's over

69. Ask yourself questions

70. Stay connected

71. Move things around before buying something new

72. Think like a film director

73. Begin from within

74. Paint, if you can't redecorate

75. Have a clear vision

76. Love twos

77. Love threes

78. Bring outdoor fabric in

79. Return to the classics

80. Change is good

81. Turn off the television

82. Silence your cell phone

83. Want to be alone

84. Stare at the horizon

85. Take short rests throughout your day

86. Treat your time as money

87. Walk slowly

88. Cherish contrast

89. Put your feet up

90. Go more slowly

91. Take time to ground yourself

92. Write it down

93. Drive

94. Regularly hit the stop button

95. Think before acting

96. Contemplate

97. Explore your options, then choose

98. Relish early Sunday mornings

99. Go ahead: decide

100. Have fun

ACKNOWLEDGEMENTS

First and foremost, my eternal gratitude to my Teacher and for my path.

Heartfelt thanks to Peter Namdev Hayes for his guidance and editorial support, Uma Patti Hayes for her copy editing, the team at *Epigraph* and *Monkfish Publishing*, Marc and Jenna Friedenthal, Robbyn Footlick, Melissa Ausburn, Mia Pepin, John Esposito, Jeremy Rizzi, Billy Armas, Michael Scaven, Seth Lemoine, Elka Boren, Youngja Yoo, Leigh Rappaport, Sanchi Gillett, Shridevi Boily, Nick Carlstrom, Robin Kramer, Jack Lynch, Laura Lee Miller, Jennifer Masella, Jack Wettling, Mitchell Karsch, Filipek Arkadiusz, Sheldon Kasowitz, Sammy Chadwick, Bruni Musikant, Kenny Wapner, Dan and Bianca Harris, Margie Connelly, Jennifer Lameroux, Regina Livers, Anne Kitchens, Suzanne Levine, Vera Wang, Janet League Katzin, Josh Gelder, Gregg Soloman, Elie Tahari, Apollonia Fortuna, Tracy Coffie, Laura Harrington, Irina Belykh-Conching, Leila Lemoine, Sandy Walker, Gavin Adair, Christian Quaritius, Charles Fagan, Angela Patterson, Soraya Gomez Crawford, Max Wilson, Kevin Meconi, Josephine Esposito, Jorge Suarez Jr, Elaine and Bill Crudo, Peter and Cathy Ladd, Monicka Hanssen Téele, David

Brody, Michael Paurowski, Patricia Hills, Lorena Casas Borjenseen, Christine Aliverto, Frank Cassata, Denise Figlar Wilson, Peter Brown, Gregory Clouatre, Terry Fleming, Diane Eichenbaum, Liz Kirschner, Tony LoGrande, Christopher Makos, Paul Solberg, Genevieve Moore, Richard Travers, Gregg Pellegrini, Natasha Phillips, Christian Quaritius, Amy Sandler Tezak, Cory Shields, April Singer, Veronica Tao Chevalier, Calvin Klein, Stuart Marmorstein and Richard Hastings.

And much love and many thanks to my family: Emilio and Emily Calica, Carl and Rosamon Calica, Marcus, Miguel and Maxwell Calica.

ABOUT THE AUTHOR

K evin Calica is a New York-based designer and visual artist, whose clients are some of the world's leading brands. Kevin was influenced at an early age by the Shaker aesthetic and the writings of Henry David Thoreau. He apprenticed with Ralph Lauren and, at Calvin Klein Inc., was the youngest vice-president in the history of the company. His "strong and simple" signature style can be seen at www.strengthandsimplicity.com. A born teacher, he offers classes on visual merchandising and fashion marketing at Parsons School of Design.

"If anyone knows about how to live beautifully and comfortably, it's Kevin Calica. The years we worked together were always inspirational. Kevin is a true artist and innovator. This book is a must read!"

—Calvin Klein

CPSIA information can be obtained at www.ICGtesting.com
Printed in the USA
LVOW12s0922011113

359429LV00005B/30/P